C000017859

DON'T WORRY, WE HAVE SOME NUTS FOR YOU

DON'T YOU FEEL WEAK?

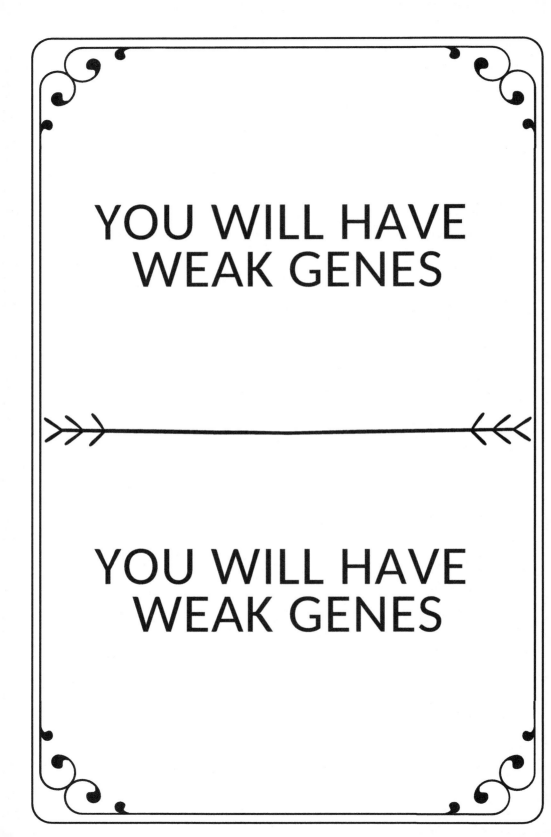

TODAY VEGE
TOMORROW HOMO

AREN'T YOU WORRY THAT YOU
WILL DIE BECAUSE OF THAT?

THE MEAT YOU EAT IS
ALREADY DEAD, SO YOU
WON'T CHANGE ANYTHING

>>>———————————<<<

YOU HAVE LOSS YOUR HAIR

OH MY GOD, ONCE A
WEEK IS NOT A SIN

I WILL GIVE YOU 50$ IF
YOU EAT THIS TURKEY

BUT WHAT DO YOU EAT?

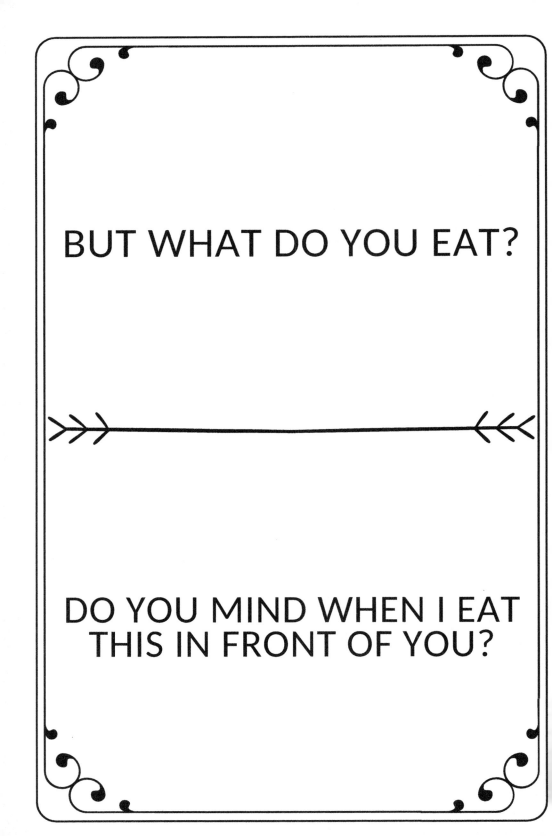

DO YOU MIND WHEN I EAT
THIS IN FRONT OF YOU?

LET ME FEED YOU

CAN'T YOU PICK THE MEAT OUT OR JUST EAT AROUND IT?

ANIMALS ARE ON EARTH
FOR SOME REASON

WANT A BITE?

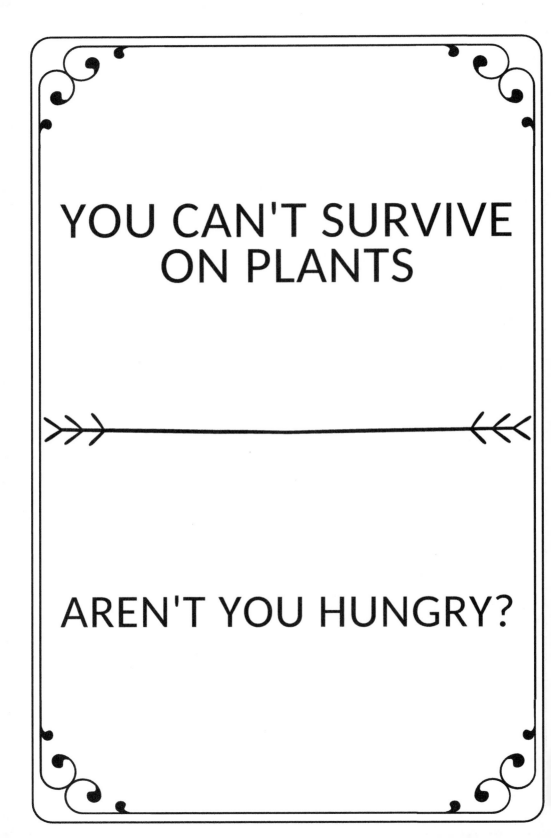

YOU CAN'T SURVIVE
ON PLANTS

AREN'T YOU HUNGRY?

TOFU IS PROBABLY YOUR
SECOND NAME NOW

>>>————————————————————<<<

SO WHAT DO YOU
ACTUALLY EAT?

DO YOU EVER CHEAT?

ISN'T THAT CHICKEN LOOKING DELICIOUS?

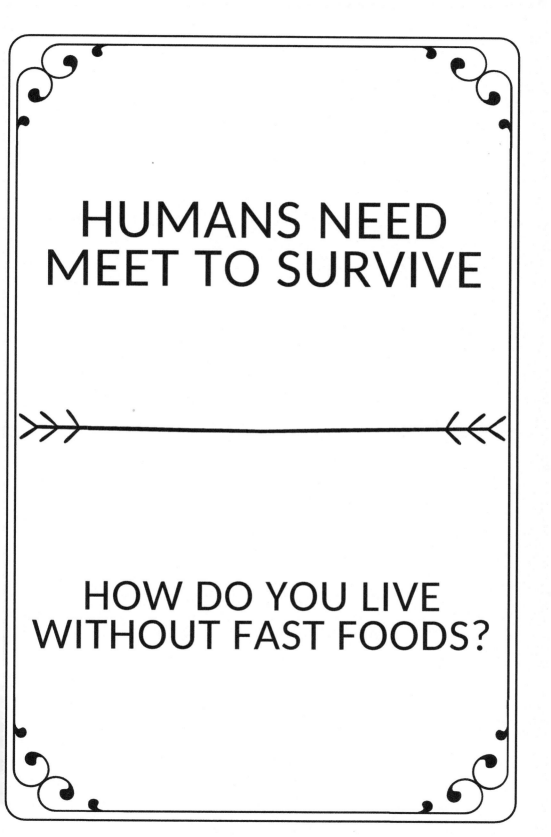

HUMANS NEED MEET TO SURVIVE

HOW DO YOU LIVE WITHOUT FAST FOODS?

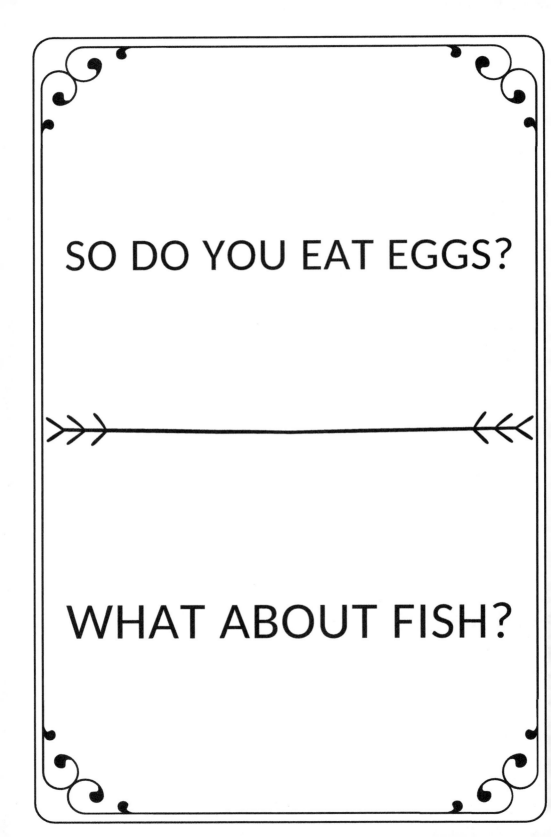

SO DO YOU EAT EGGS?

WHAT ABOUT FISH?

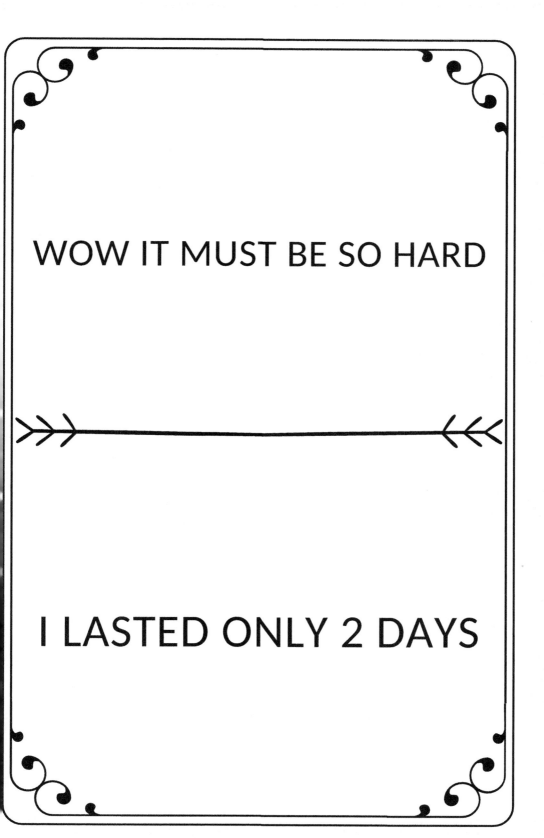

DO YOU EVEN LIKE VEGETABLES?

AREN'T YOU A HIPPY?

FOR MORAL OR HEALTH REASONS?

HAVE YOU SEEN SOME DOCUMENTARY ON THAT?

GOD DAMN IT, JUST TAKE ONE BITE

>>>———————————————————<<<

HUMANS WERE MADE TO EAT MEAT

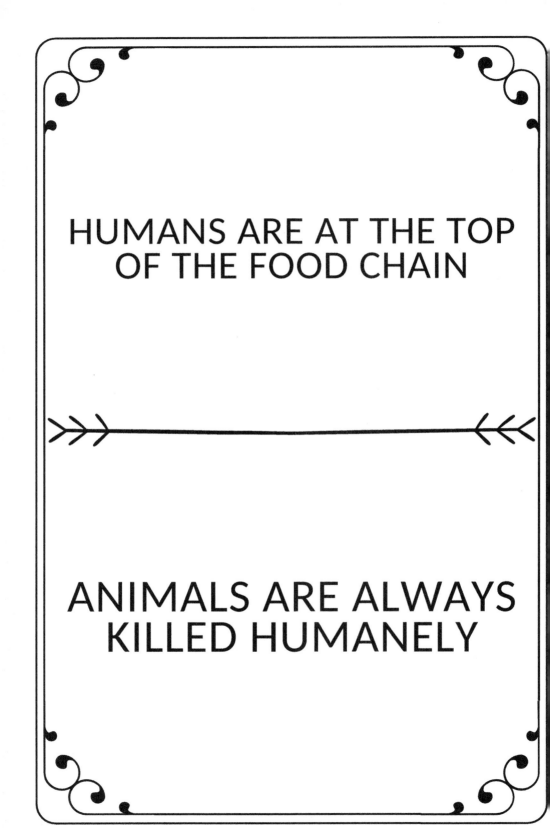

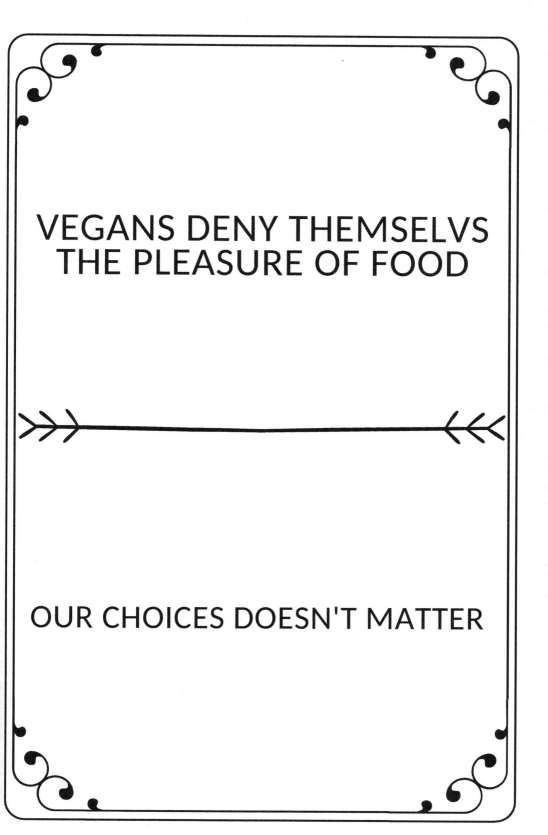

VEGANS DENY THEMSELVS
THE PLEASURE OF FOOD

OUR CHOICES DOESN'T MATTER

IF YOU WERE ON A DESERT ISLAND AND ONLY HAD THE OPTION OF EATING MEAT TO SURVIVE, WOULD YOU?

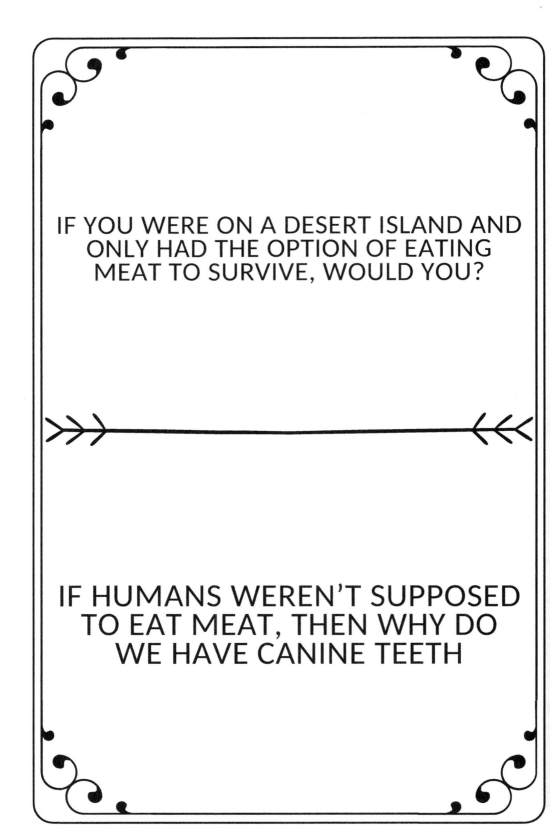

IF HUMANS WEREN'T SUPPOSED TO EAT MEAT, THEN WHY DO WE HAVE CANINE TEETH

IT'S TRADITION TO EAT
TURKEY ON THANKSGIVING

WHY DO YOU HAVE
TO BE DIFFICULT

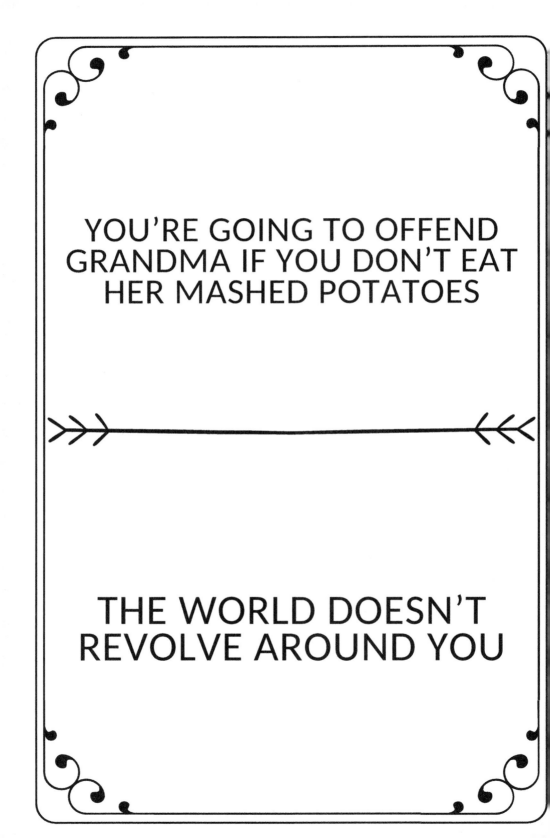

YOU'RE GOING TO OFFEND
GRANDMA IF YOU DON'T EAT
HER MASHED POTATOES

THE WORLD DOESN'T
REVOLVE AROUND YOU

IT MUST BE REALLY BORING

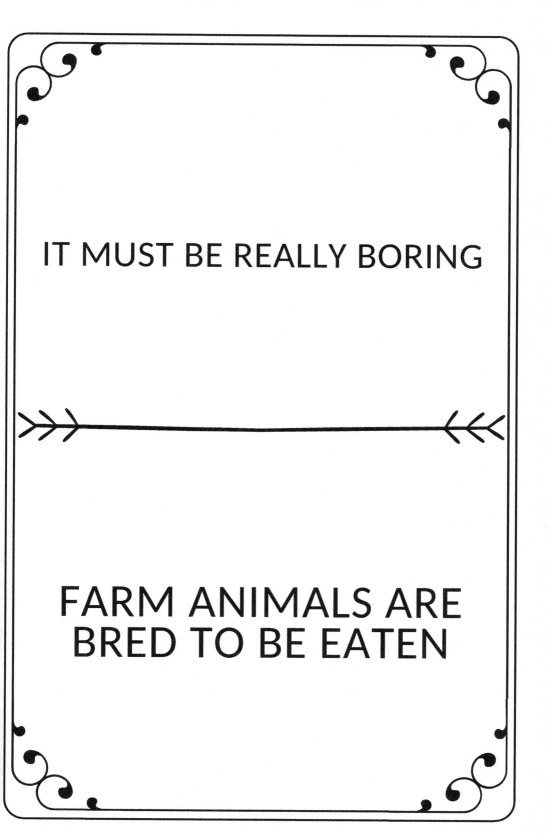

FARM ANIMALS ARE
BRED TO BE EATEN

CAN'T YOU JUST EAT THIS ONE
NON-VEGAN THING TODAY?
NOTHING WILL HAPPEN TO YOU

DO YOU HATE ME FOR
BEING A CARNIVORE?

IF YOU ARE A VEGETARIAN
YOU MUST BE INTENSE

>>>————————————————<<<

VEGETARIANS ALWAYS
COMPLAIN ABOUT
EVERYTHING

DO YOU FEEL LIKE YOU'RE BETTER THAN EVERYONE ELSE

VEGETARIANS ARE ALWAYS TALKING ABOUT BEING VEGETARIANS

BEING A VEGETARIAN IS JUST A TREND

I HATE THAT VEGETARIANS ARE ALWAYS TRYING TO CONVERT ME

BEING A VEGETARIAN IS TOO EXPENSIVE

I'VE THOUGHT ABOUT EATING LESS MEAT, BUT GOING VEGETARIAN IS JUST TOO EXTREME

DID YOU KNOW THAT HUMAN BEINGS EVOLVED BECAUSE OF MEAT?

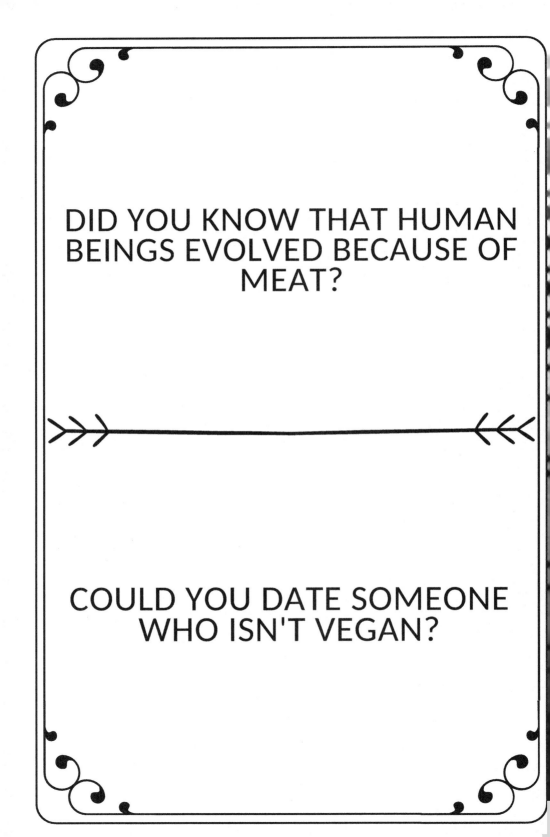

COULD YOU DATE SOMEONE WHO ISN'T VEGAN?

WHAT IF YOU CRAVE MEAT
WHEN YOU ARE PREGNANT?

I FEEL LIKE VEGAN
FOOD IS WEIRD

YOU'RE NOT A REAL MAN

WOULDN'T A COW EXPLODE
IF YOU STOPPED MILKING IT

WHAT IF SOMEONE GAVE YOU A MILLION DOLLARS, WOULD YOU EAT A PIECE OF MEAT

CAN YOU DRINK ALCOHOL?

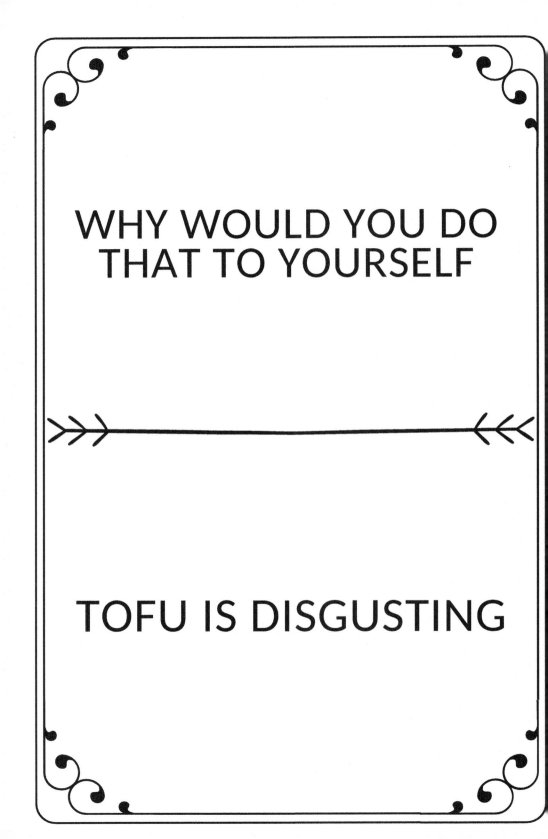

WHY WOULD YOU DO
THAT TO YOURSELF

TOFU IS DISGUSTING

I CAN'T AFFORD TO
BE VEGETARIAN

WILL YOU MAKE YOUR
KIDS EAT VEGAN TOO?

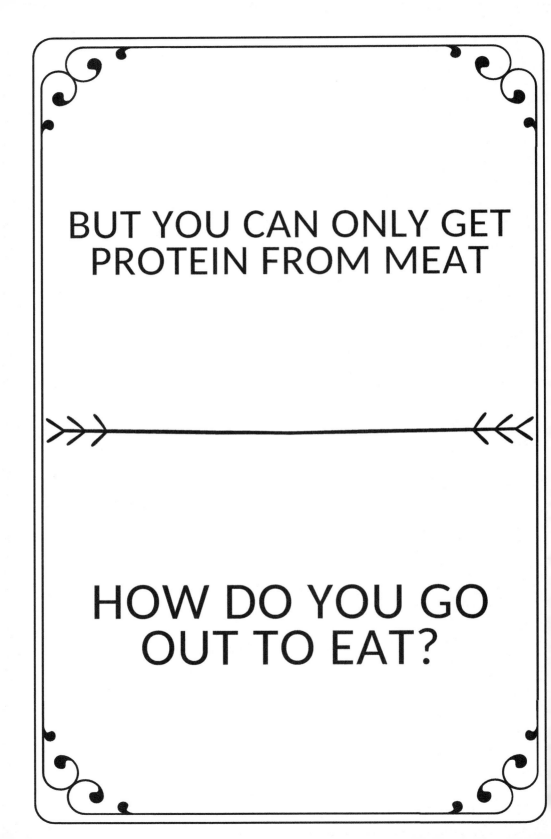

BUT YOU CAN ONLY GET PROTEIN FROM MEAT

HOW DO YOU GO OUT TO EAT?

IS THAT ALL YOU'RE EATING? I DON'T WANT YOU TO STARVE

>>>———————————————<<<

I UNDERSTAND THE ENVIRONMENTAL ASPECT BUT IT'S NOT ENOUGH TO MAKE ME GO EAT THAT WAY

WOW, I FEEL BAD FOR YOU

AREN'T YOU TIRED ALL THE TIME?

SO, WHY DID YOU DECIDE TO
BECOME A VEGETARIAN

DO YOU JUST SIT AROUND
AND EAT SALADS ALL DAY

SO IF I PUT SOME MEAT IN FRONT OF YOU RIGHT NOW, WHAT WOULD YOU DO?

BUT DAIRY ANIMALS AREN'T KILLED

YOU ARE CRAZY

THE ONLY VEGETARIAN OPTION
I HAVE IS THIS VEGGIE PLATTER.

WILL THAT WORK FOR YOU?